FOR

I THINK YOU'D ENJOY THIS BOOK BECAUSE

FROM

PRINCIPLES FOR THE NEXT CENTURY OF WORK

Sense & Respond Press publishes short, beautiful, actionable books on topics related to innovation, digital transformation, product management, and design. Our readers are smart, busy, practical innovators. Our authors are experts working in the fields they write about.

The goal of every book in our series is to solve a real-world problem for our readers. Whether that be understanding a complex and emerging topic, or something as concrete (and difficult) as hiring innovation leaders, our books help working professionals get better at their jobs, quickly.

Jeff Gothelf & Josh Seiden

Series co-editors **Jeff Gothelf** and **Josh Seiden** wrote *Lean UX* (O'Reilly) and *Sense & Respond* (Harvard Business Review Press) together. They were co-founding principals of Neo Innovation (sold to Pivotal Labs) in New York City and helped build it into one of the most recognized brands in modern product strategy, development, and design. In 2017 they were short-listed for the Thinkers50 award for their contributions to innovation leadership. Learn more about Jeff and Josh at www.jeffgothelf.com and www.joshseiden.com.

OTHER BOOKS FROM SENSE & RESPOND PRESS

Lean vs. Agile vs. Design Thinking
What you really need to know to build high-performing digital product teams
Jeff Gothelf

Making Progress
The 7 responsibilities of the innovation leader
Ryan Jacoby

Hire Women
An Agile framework for hiring and retaining women in technology
Debbie Madden

Hiring for the Innovation Economy
Three steps to improve performance and diversity
Nicole Rufuku

The Invisible Leader (forthcoming)
Facilitation secrets for catalyzing change, cultivating innovation, and commanding results
Elena Astilleros

What CEOs Need to Know about Design (forthcoming)
Using design to grow revenue and maximize strategic impact
Audrey Crane

To keep up with new releases or submit book ideas to the press check out our website at www.senseandrespondpress.com

LATERAL LEADERSHIP

Copyright © 2018 by Tim Herbig

All rights reserved. No part of this publication may be reproduced, stored in a retrieval system, or transmitted, in any form or by any means, electronic, mechanical, photocopying, recording, or otherwise, without the prior written permission of the publisher.

Issued in print and electronic formats.
ISBN 978-1-7292049-3-1 (KDP paperback)
ISBN 978-1-7328184-0-8 (ebook)

Editor: Victoria Olsen
Designer: Mimi O Chun
Interior typesetting: Jennifer Blais
Author photograph: Sebastian Friedrich Bentzi

Published in the United States by Sense & Respond Press
www.senseandrespondpress.com

Printed and bound in the United States.
1 2 3 4   20 19 18 17

Tim Herbig

LATERAL LEADERSHIP

A practical guide for Agile product managers

INTRODUCTION

We're entering a future in which companies need to be structured based on loosely-connected and self-organized agile teams instead of static silos—but this organizational transformation has created a crisis in leadership. When autonomous teams work together side by side, who is in charge? A new challenge arises for individual contributors: leading teams without hierarchical power, or *lateral leadership*.

Lateral leadership is a critical skill for our age. In fact, it must become a core responsibility for one of the most important roles emerging in business today: product management. Product managers typically operate at the intersection of business, technology, and user experience in order to deliver a product that is valuable, usable, and feasible. Product managers get called a lot of things, from "Mini CEOs" to "Jacks of all trades" all the way down to "Ticket Monkeys." The list of responsibilities attached to this job is considerably longer than all available nicknames combined.

But an often-times overlooked responsibility is people leadership: guiding others as a peer at eye-level instead of coming from above, "blessed" with the fairy dust of a C-level executive. This is a demanding challenge for generalists who are often tasked with leading incredibly sharp domain experts without being perceived as micromanagers—and without the seeming safety net of hierarchical power. On a company level, the tendency to religiously stick to given agile frameworks can become a trap. There is a strong temptation to focus on the process side of collaboration and neglect the interpersonal side, which creates an emotional intelligence vacuum for lateral leaders to suffer in.

I know how important lateral leadership is based on hard-won personal experience. A pivotal moment for me was a situation I encountered three years into my job as a product manager. I had a discussion about goals with another designer on the team, based on a suggestion she made. After exchanging arguments, I left the conversation thinking that I had made it clear why her proposal was not relevant at that moment, based on the mission briefing we had committed to. However, when we then had a meeting with our boss, she brought it up for discussion again, leaving me with the impression that she didn't respect the decision I made earlier on. In addition, this obvious conflict between us caused my boss to question whether I was able to lead the team as a product manager responsible for the outcome.

The incident illustrated an element that wasn't a part of the regular certification workshops for product managers, which I thought was all I needed to know about how "Agile" worked. I then realized how little I knew about lateral leadership—and how much I needed to learn beyond the processes of the most common agile practices like Kanban or Scrum. Kanban is a work prioritization method pioneered by Toyota in Japan. It's designed to limit work in progress, visualize the overall workflow, and identify bottlenecks to efficiency. Scrum, on the other hand, focuses on achieving goals which were set by the team within a given period of time called Sprints (e.g. two weeks). Every Sprint should produce a potentially releasable artifact for customers, helping teams to iterate towards a bigger product in small steps.

Leading a cross-functional agile team means more than monitoring the team's work using Gantt charts or micromanaging how they produce results. It means not feeling completely lost when the re-prioritization decision you recently made gets undermined by a snarky comment in the standup. It means addressing the annoyance you may feel when the designer yet again "forgot" to create the set of design versions you asked for and didn't look at the competitor examples you shared. And it also means carefully managing relationships and conflicts with peers on other teams. It's about how to deal with the mix of fear and anger you feel when your lead engineer openly criticizes your decisions in front of your business unit head. All those situations hurt your ability to achieve your goals. They are the result of poor alignment between you, your stakeholders, and the entire team.

This book will define what it takes to master the challenges of being a lateral leader, guiding you through chapters on strategic alignment with your team and individual alignment with other team members. Chapters on empathy and escalation provide tools to maintain and strengthen your leadership role within agile teams. Throughout the book I focus primarily on the struggles a product manager must overcome when acting as a lateral leader. This is not a dissection of theoretical traditional leadership principles or the psychological frameworks you get taught in "leadership trainings." Instead, I will share first-person stories from my many years of experience in product management and provide hands-on advice for your daily work through the Activities sections at the end of each chapter.

    Most importantly, don't treat this book as a step-by-step strategy you have to power through from the first to the last suggested activity. Instead, get going within any part of it and, after some practice, you'll be able to mix-and-match activities for new situations and contexts.

"AGILE DOESN'T HAVE A BRAIN:" HOW TO LEAD WITHOUT HIERARCHICAL LEADERSHIP

When you take over the role of a product manager as part of an agile team, it takes a while to realize what's expected of you. Besides owning the product from a customer and stakeholder perspective, you're also expected to lead an entire team of extremely sharp domain experts as well. But you were probably never asked in an interview about your experience leading people and you probably never saw this requirement in your job description.

As Bill Scott, a VP of Product at PayPal, put it, "Agile doesn't have a brain," which is why even people who work in agile environments for years sometimes feel lost in it. While the quote originally refers to the agnostic perspective Agile takes towards the topic being worked on, I think it also shows that agile methodologies leave a vacuum when it comes to leadership within teams. Sometime between burning Gantt charts to celebrate the end of waterfall projects and handing out planning poker cards, we forget that Agile means more than shipping software earlier and faster.

In fact, the first principle of the Agile Manifesto places "individuals and interactions" over "processes and tools." But that means more than just asking teams to collaborate. As organizational coach Christina Wodtke notes, "bringing a group of people into a room isn't enough to make them a team. An effective team requires personal connections and psychological safety." All the best intentions in the world won't lead us anywhere if we don't pay attention to the way we interact with each other beyond the bullet points in our job descriptions.

Because Agile deliberately excludes top-down management thinking from the way we build products, it's time to remove managerial leadership tools like performance improvement plans and written warnings as well. While these disciplinary measures were the backbone of traditional management, they are not suitable for environments where people operate as equal peers and they have a major flaw: they assume people have little to no intrinsic motivation to do their job well. Instead, according to this view, employees need the right amount of external pressure to perform and achieve their goals. Written warnings were meant to remind them to never repeat a mistake again (because it was assumed they wouldn't pay attention otherwise).

The takeaway: we can't simply start applying new ways of working in the form of agile principles without questioning the way we lead at the same time.

The good news: it's not your fault. It's the result of the way organizations have understood and designed leadership so far.

IMPLICIT VS. EXPLICIT LEADERSHIP

Gary Hamel, the American management expert, offers this great quote summarizing the imbalance between business and management practices:

> "Right now, your company has 21st century Internet enabled business processes, mid-20th century management processes, all built atop 19th century management principles."

While this quote is primarily directed at hierarchical managers to rethink their approach to leadership, I think it holds a lot of truth for lateral leaders as well.

Typically, there are two ways to lead within most companies.

First is what I like to call "explicit" leadership. This refers to jobs featuring titles like "Head of," "Director," or "VP." These positions carry formal authority right in their names. People filling these roles have hierarchical responsibility for a group of people, so you either need to have practical experience in leading people or you had training for it. In these cases, the word "lead" can be found numerous times in the "responsibilities" and "required skills" area of your job description. In fact, when you enter a meeting room, there's a fair chance that some people in there have to report to you simply due to hierarchy.

The second type of leadership is much less visible because so much is going on beneath the surface: this can be called "implicit" leadership. Implicit leadership roles don't automatically come with hierarchical power attached to them; yet they are still part of the role of an individual contributor, often combined with a "junior" or "senior" prefix. The critical difference is that leadership skills are often-times not within the required set of skills or experiences for one of these roles, and you may have no clear hierarchical cues. However, in the case of a product manager, leading is a significant part of the job. Even on a team of equals, someone must own the outcome of a project or orchestrate collaboration among domain experts. That responsibility unfortunately may only be recognized on the job and not yet be part of hiring and training processes—but it's no less real.

This leads to the problem for agile teams I described in the Introduction: a pattern where there are specific expectations for the team's outcomes, but no recognition of the necessary leadership skills, tools, and training to achieve those outcomes.

ENTER LATERAL LEADERSHIP

While the lack of hierarchical authority seems like a loss of power to most newly-appointed lateral leaders, I encourage you to see it as an opportunity because it enables you to rethink leadership entirely—without the burden of traditional management thinking. Traditional management mostly happened on the business side of interpersonal relationships and focused on performance metrics and allocated training budgets. Managers were encouraged to neglect seemingly softer aspects like empathy and compassion for two major reasons:

First, top levels of organizations have usually been dominated by men, who displayed stereotypically male-associated characteristics like assertiveness or courage when managing others. And because skills like empathy or compassion are primarily associated with the way women are supposed to act and feel, we've only seen these gaining recognition as more women rise through all levels of hierarchy in organizations.

Second, demonstrating empathy towards each other requires opening up and becoming vulnerable. Vulnerability has for a long time been considered unprofessional in work relationships, let alone across hierarchies.

But as a lateral leader, you have to think beyond these assumptions. Due to your implicit leadership role, you can't rely on the impact of hierarchical measures for leading others. It's your job to recognize and leverage empathy across domains and individuals while still aligning team members and peers on a strategic level.

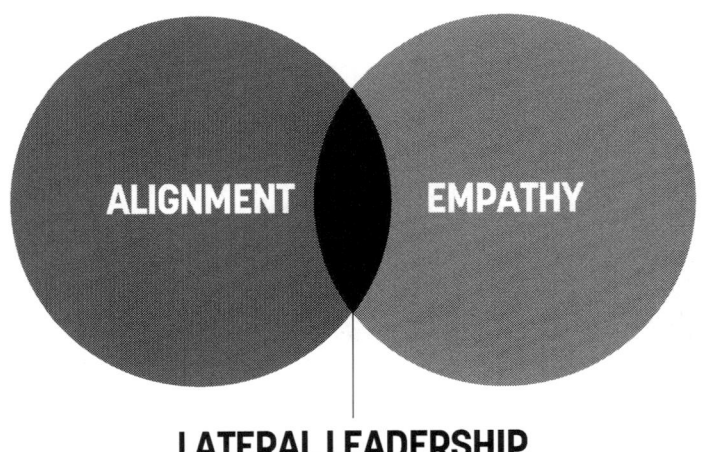

Lateral Leadership happens at the intersection of Alignment and Empathy.

Alignment takes care of the more objective and process-side of things (making sure we have clarity on the goal and what needs to be done). Empathy, however, focuses on the individual, his or her struggles, and how to raise awareness for the challenges within a domain of expertise.

If you're thinking that lateral leadership doesn't apply to you, for whatever reasons, I challenge you to think again. Influencing others without formal authority is a trait needed at small startups and large corporates alike. However, while both alignment and empathy are equally important, they need to be prioritized differently based on your work environment.

In small-scale startups, everybody collaborates so closely without hierarchies that alignment gaps are not one of the biggest problems. Instead, interpersonal relationships are critical and therefore need a lot of empathy to function well.

In large corporations, strategic alignment is the key to agile teams effectively collaborating across departments. Creating empathy still has a high priority, but when you tackle it depends on the organizational maturity of your company.

Let's put it this way: while alignment manages the questions coming from our brain/head, empathy is about listening to our heart and gut. And as always in life, it's about striking the right balance.

Note: One way to synchronize leadership with agile methodologies could be through servant leadership, which is characterized by putting yourself last. This book will not dissect servant leadership because I don't consider it a primary tool for lateral leaders. From my perspective, servant leadership is much better suited for the role of the Scrum Master or Agile Coach. If you want to learn more about this approach, I recommend you take a look at Servant Leadership: A Journey into the Nature of Legitimate Power and Greatness *by Robert K. Greenleaf and Larry C. Spears.*

This book also won't cover agile processes directly, though building ground rules for the process side of things is important and should not be ignored. There is a ton of writing out there from smart people on how to design effective team processes. For a primer on how to design effective agile processes (e.g. within Scrum) I recommend looking at the unofficial Scrum checklist from the former Agile Coach at Spotify, Henrik Kniberg. And if you're looking for processes beyond the core definition of Agile, I recommend the writing of the organizational development expert Christina Wodtke. In it, you will find useful hints ranging from how to create a Team Charter to manage feedback among peers. (See my Reading List at the end of the book for these and other useful resources.)

ACTIVITIES

Recognize your lateral leadership environment
» Write down the names of all the people you have asked to fulfill a request for you in the past 30 days.
» Perform the "vacation day test" with every one of them: are you the one person granting or rejecting that peer's vacation days? If not, you are or you have been in a lateral leadership relationship with them. In other words, you need to think about how to influence them without formal authority.

Assess your current state of lateral leadership skills
» Ask the people around you (from the list created above) to rate your skills in creating alignment and demonstrating empathy when interacting with you (on a simple scale of 1 to 5 with 1 being the lowest level and 5 indicating you're meeting their expectations). Sample questions:

- » "How do you rate my ability to create alignment in terms of a shared understanding about what needs to be achieved?"
- » "How to you rate my ability to demonstrate empathy towards the people I work with on a regular basis?"
» Then ask them to name specific situations in which you succeeded or failed.

Locate your blind spots
» Put those people on a scale according to how often you interact with them, with 1 being the least often and 5 being the most often. Focus on improving your interactions with the people you interact with most.

STRATEGIC ALIGNMENT: HOW TO MAKE SURE EVERYBODY FOLLOWS YOUR VISION

Strategic alignment gaps can be spotted when there's a mismatch in what people are actually doing, compared to what a lateral leader expected them to do.

Let's say you kicked-off a new product initiative. You'll need to validate the problem and design and discuss multiple aspects of a potential solution with the engineering team. After all, your job is to provide the right guidance to allow the experts on your team to do their job. But when you revisit the current state of discussion, you recognize that the team is focused on parts of the solution that are actually secondary to the overall success of the project. Most likely, this isn't just due to confusion but due to a lack of alignment about what needs to be done.

SPECIFIC PATTERNS TO WATCH OUT FOR:

» The priorities of the overall goal are not reflected in people's day-to-day actions: such as when at least two-thirds of the capacity of a sprint is not spent on the highest priority epic.
» Team members and lateral peers perceive you as a micromanager. While micromanagement is often seen as a character trait, in fact it's just a natural reaction to poor alignment. This means it's not about changing the people, but tackling the alignment processes on a higher level.

All of your teammates and most of your peers come from different mindsets and have their own perspectives on an initiative or product. In order to ensure that everybody works in the right direction, you need to find a way to translate those perspectives into a format that is neutral enough to be understood even by outsiders, but also carries enough passion and inspiration to make everybody follow through.

The traditional way of closing alignment gaps has been to add more detail to the conversation: more detailed control, more detailed information, and more detailed instructions. From the perspective of a product manager, this might have meant adding more detailed requirements to the tickets in your backlog or checking in way too often on the work that designers or developers are doing. From the perspective of a traditional manager, it meant telling employees exactly what they needed to do and how. What gets forgotten in those conversations is the *why*. It gets reduced to a side note as leaders direct peers and teammates so closely that they don't have a chance of missing the goal.

With the rise of agile teams (which, remember, are based on the concept of autonomy) this approach is set up to fail: it's just impossible for lateral leaders to tell individuals or groups of domain experts how they should solve a problem step-by-step because they lack the required expertise. Or have you seen product managers providing specs for which frontend framework to pick and how a transition between views should behave? Their team would push back against such interference by the third retrospective at the latest.

Paradoxically, laterally-led peers demand even more autonomy to focus on their respective craft. Lateral leaders have to ensure their teams make progress toward their goals. They also have to do this with as little hands-on management as possible to avoid creating the impression of micromanagement, which leads to resistance.

So how do you achieve that mission impossible?

MEET THE MISSION BRIEFING

The strategy consultant Stephen Bungay originally described a core alignment element called the mission briefing in his book *The Art of Action*. In it, Bungay shows how military leaders set up their subordinates for success in the field, without narrowing their choice of options. Strategically, these leaders couldn't micromanage their teams in the field; instead, they had to enable them to perform at their very best when their leaders were not present.

Overall, Bungay's mission briefing can be summarized into three directives:
- » Give individuals freedom to adjust their actions in line with intent.
- » Limit direction to defining and communicating the intent.
- » Allow each level to define how they will achieve the intent of the next level up, and "back brief" so all involved parties are aware of any new changes.

Bungay's concept has been adopted and refined by many product organizations, but let's look at one practical iteration, which I adapted slightly for product managers. It has five parts and unfolds its true impact on alignment when co-created by the entire team.

FIRST, WRITE DOWN THE CONTEXT YOUR TEAM WORKS IN.
Here you should describe the situation your product and/or your market is in, in an objective way. Gather all the facts that would make an external observer understand the status quo and what change led to an initiative like yours. Some questions to answer when writing this section could be:
- » What are the (changed) internal and external circumstances that trigger this initiative, such as the user or business problem?
- » How do you know that this is a good opportunity to spend time, people, and money on?

For the sake of practicality, let's assume we're an ecommerce company selling goods on our own website. As the product manager, you're trying to align everybody on your idea of extending your website to enable automated selling on platforms like Amazon or eBay.

In this scenario, bullet points of your context could look something like this:
- » Our Year over Year (YoY) revenue growth has slowed down recently to 3% (from 10% the year before and 15% before that).
- » There's an overall trend towards selling on platforms compared to focusing on own shops.
- » The YoY revenue growth of Amazon and eBay have accelerated for the tenth year in a row.
- » Surveys have shown that our former customers now shop instead at Amazon, citing "free and fast shipping" and "I'm there anyway to buy groceries" as the primary reasons.
- » Our current shop system is only built for displaying and updating items in our own shop.
- » Manually adding our entire catalogue would take about 900 work days of category managers in total and about three work days per new item.

SECOND, EXPLAIN THE HIGHER INTENT.

While this section is often-times seen as the place to put a CEO quote, it's important for you as a leader to show your peers where their efforts fit in with the big picture—ie. the vision, mission, and strategy of the company. So, the (seemingly) simple question to answer here is "How does this align with our overall mission and strategy?"

In our example case, we could answer something like this:
- » "Always be where our customers are" is the leading principle for our product development efforts to achieve our company goal of double digit YoY revenue growth.

THIRD, DETAIL MY INTENT.

Here's where you motivate your peers to follow you on this journey. You want to simplify the complications of real life and enable your peers to act by giving them an overall purpose: it is an insight into the essentials. Think about how to make the link to the higher intent visible as well.

> One intent we could state as part of our example is:
> » Automatically make our inventory available on other shopping platforms without additional cost, increasing revenue growth.

While this statement is the qualitative aspect of your intent, you have to strengthen it with a quantitative measure to give your team a metric to aim for (similar to the OKR concept).

> » Generate $500,000 of revenue from purchases from eBay and Amazon within six months after launch.

FOURTH, NOTE KEY IMPLIED TASKS.

Don't get confused by the title. It's not about writing a step-by-step playbook for your team on how to execute this project (remember how domain experts resist people stepping into their fields?). Instead, outline what kind of outcomes your team needs to achieve along the way so that working towards them can be divided and assigned further.

Examples:

> » Understand limitations and similarities of Amazon and eBay APIs.
> » Identify most desired categories from our catalogue by customers on Amazon and eBay.

FIFTH, DEFINE BOUNDARIES.

Here we can add the right kind of guard rails for the creative playground we want our peers to fill. It's about stating what we explicitly won't do as part of this project and what is not allowed to happen as a side effect. Metrics like this are often-times also called Key Failure Indicators (KFI), which are metrics you don't want to see go in a certain direction as part of this initiative. KFIs are meant to counter the main KPI of the project for a healthy balance, ie. "Grow revenue while maintaining gross margin."

Looking back at our example case, we could put in something like:
- » Prices of our items on Amazon and eBay are not allowed to be more than 5% cheaper than in our own shop.
- » We won't deliver items to Rakuten or Wish as part of this initiative.

My personal litmus test for how aligned I am with my peers when having worked on a mission briefing document includes two questions to them. You can say these questions out loud when actually talking to your peers but I also repeat them in my head when writing my first draft:
- » "Alright, so the mission briefing is settled enough that I can share this one level up and add that we're committed, right?"
- » "Ok, so I could go on vacation tomorrow for the next eight weeks and you'd have everything you need to work on this, right?"

Ultimately, that's what it's about: providing just enough guidance to enable the team to answer questions they may encounter along the way—but without settling on narrow specifics that could limit their creativity to find the best solutions.

The professional network XING adopted Bungay's idea of the mission briefing for their own organizational challenges. Organized in cross-functional business units and with more than twenty dedicated product teams, product managers at XING often struggled with achieving two critical aspects of their work: the autonomy they wanted for executing a product vision from their bosses and the commitment for team capacities from other units they depended on.

XING defined the motivation behind creating an alignment tool as follows:

> Autonomy is not something you claim—it's something you can only earn through successful alignment with stakeholders, peers and within your team.
>
> We believe that good alignment should be a collaborative effort during which
> 1. The tricky questions about an upcoming initiative are discussed early
> 2. The underlying thinking of an initiative is sharpened for clarity of intent
> 3. The results are made transparent to get everyone "on the same page"

The XING version of the mission briefing, called *Auftragsklärung*, quickly became one of the key talking points for new projects. Auftragsklärung is a framework for collaborative alignment that can be used in large product organizations as well as in other contexts such as client/agency setups. While it was first introduced as a mandatory measure from upper management, most product managers soon started to recognize the value in articulating thoughts in a concise and structured format.

It's tempting to look at the cornerstones of a mission briefing and think, "Why should I write it down? This stuff is so obvious and I mentioned this part and that part just lately over lunch with the team." This is one of the key lessons of strategic alignment: you can never be too explicit about it. While you may indeed have dropped one or the other sentence over lunch, each of your teammates puts it in a different context. And depending on their drivers and motivators, they get more or less intrigued by it.

In a past project, I made exactly that mistake. I thought our goal was all clear to my team and also didn't put in the work to modify an existing mission briefing with my own words when it was time to inspire a new vision. Instead, we just carried along and the question of our final goal (ie. when would we be successful?) was never really clear, nor had we the committed resources from other departments we depended on (ie. we were missing lateral alignment with other product teams).

Naturally, a couple of weeks into this unclear situation we arrived at a critical tipping point for both the project itself and my leadership role for this team. With the help of my former Team Lead Engineering and Scrum Master, I orchestrated a two-day boot camp with the core team and participating stakeholders. In it, we walked through and iterated the mission briefing once more, to reflect our own new perspective.

After that, we made the results as visible as possible in our team area to remind everybody of that shared understanding. And even though there were still unanswered questions about how much capacity we would be able to receive from other development teams, we at least got the conversation started and had a solid foundation for it.

REMEMBER: ALIGNMENT DOESN'T MEAN AGREEMENT

The purpose of a mission briefing is to develop a shared understanding of what needs to be done and why. It's not to make everybody happy. Often I see people confusing alignment with agreement. Jeff Bezos explained the difference in his 2016 Letter to Shareholders:

> Use the phrase "disagree and commit." This phrase will save a lot of time. If you have conviction on a particular direction even though there's no consensus, it's helpful to say, "Look, I know we disagree on this but will you gamble with me on it? Disagree and commit?" By the time you're at this point, no one can know the answer for sure, and you'll probably get a quick yes.
>
> This isn't one way.
>
> If you're the boss, you should do this too. I disagree and commit all the time. We recently greenlit a particular Amazon Studios original. I told the team my view: debatable whether it would be interesting enough, complicated to produce, the business terms aren't that good, and we have lots of other opportunities. They had a completely different opinion and wanted to go ahead. I wrote back right away with "I disagree and commit and hope it becomes the most watched thing we've ever made." Consider how much slower this decision cycle would have been if the team had actually had to convince me rather than simply get my commitment.

See what Bezos did there? He positioned himself as a lateral leader for the Amazon Studios team instead of enforcing hierarchical power to push through his opinion.

Sell your books at World of Books!
Go to sell.worldofbooks.com and get an instant price quote. We even pay the shipping - see what your old books are worth today!

Inspected By: joanna_chavez

0008999266 1

Even if you have all relevant stakeholders and team members on board for a mission briefing, it doesn't mean that everybody shares your ideas 100%. It just means that they have committed themselves (and potentially their resources) to follow the suggested path without bringing the core principles of the project back into question week after week.

ACTIVITIES

» Consult your team and your stakeholders and choose a current or upcoming project to practice your first mission briefing. Typically, a mission briefing should cover projects that are meant to last between three and twelve months. Anything below that is probably not worth the effort and anything beyond that is too unpredictable.
» Block at least half a day for a Mission Briefing Workshop with your team and most important stakeholders. No detailed preparation is needed, but if possible, ask a fellow product manager or agile coach to facilitate the meeting, so you can focus on the content.
» Bring data about the status quo and brainstorm a potential higher intent with your boss in advance. Share the strategic input for your company/business unit to set the stage.
» Introduce the overall format to the team and walk them through every section, including the probing questions.
» Perform ideation sessions to gather perspectives, identify gaps, and make commitments to the most representative set of artifacts per section (remember, not everybody needs to get their way here).

» Discuss and commit to the final result with your boss, eventually back brief with the workshop participants, and ultimately make it visible to everybody during the daily work.

EMPATHY: HOW TO RECOGNIZE AND ADDRESS INTERPERSONAL STRUGGLES

One discovery I made rather late in my career is that alignment will only get you so far. People don't question their purpose at work or how meaningful a project is once per quarter or during the bi-weekly retrospective. They struggle with motivation every day. This leads to the half-hearted completion of given tasks and sinking morale, which makes it hard to survive the (unavoidable) downs in a project.

More importantly, team members in this state of mind will simply walk away from you (both literally and mentally) as a leader without hierarchical power. And if you're not able to identify and react to your team members' struggles, all the nodding of heads in fake agreement is worthless for making progress on your shared goals.

That's why empathy is such a critical pillar of successful lateral leadership. After all, you already demonstrated that you can align everybody on the idea of your next initiative.

As a lateral leader, you often lack the expertise most of your peers on an agile team bring to the table. And while it may feel tempting to play catch-up, the key lies in understanding the struggles your peers are facing just enough so that you can adapt your communication and behavior accordingly. In other words, don't aim to become a domain expert. Instead, understand their pain. This will benefit you in your role in two ways:

» Your peers will understand that you appreciate their challenges just enough without starting to interfere with their daily work.
» You can ask much better questions when challenging proposed solutions, which ultimately pushes the solution to a higher level.

Most people I talk to about developing and demonstrating empathy, confuse it with personality types. It's true that some people are more empathetic than others, but that's not the point here. Instead, by applying the hands-on tips and tools I'm suggesting, you will be able to bond with your peers independently from your personality.

Applying empathy will broaden your understanding of your teammates' behaviors and put their actions in a different context—causing you to rethink your judgment. Companies like the chat-based marketing platform Drift or the social media management tool Buffer have made it a habit to encourage new hires to join the customer success team during their onboarding process. And while their primary goal is to support a customer-centric mindset, there's also an (unintentional) side effect of this experience: developing empathy for your colleagues working in customer success. This doesn't necessarily mean that you have to (or should) work for a week as a full-time engineer, designer, or marketer. It simply means that one key to building empathy lies in demonstrating the willingness to get practical within the domain of your peers.

Your efforts can range from shipping your own code (if you're not a developer) to understanding the bookkeeping process for subscription revenues (if you're not an accountant). But at the same time, don't aim to match the skill level of a domain expert. This would only cause friction if it seems like micromanagement—or waste your time. Still, you'll be surprised by how much standing in your teammates' shoes, even briefly, will help you to get commitment from an individual or a whole department for your next idea. This advice for product managers also holds true for lateral leaders from all contexts: invest in learning domain knowledge skills whenever you can.

Here's one example from early in my career. My first product management job was in the publishing business, where I worked on the mobile products of a news website. My main and most critical stakeholders were the members of the editorial staff. They (often rightfully) valued the quality of their writing over the technology, which they saw as simply the vehicle delivering their brilliant ideas to more people. Back then I wrote the occasional blog post, but I didn't consider myself a writer who could credibly publish a piece on one of Germany's largest websites. But in the context of the 2012 Olympic Games I made use of my legacy as a semi-professional swimmer. I pitched an idea about putting the performance of a Chinese swimmer into context to the sports editor and he agreed. One day later, it was live on the site. While this didn't necessarily kick-off my own career as a sports editor, I was asked for two more articles that were published on the site. What I took away from this was how beneficial moving into territory way beyond my comfort zone (and original job description) could be for the mid- and long-term relationship with my peers. Whenever I started to collaborate in a new team setup it raised my awareness for potential domain-specific challenges right from the start.

At a later stage in my career, I was responsible for a cross-functional mobile development team. And while I already considered myself aware of the general challenges the developers on my team faced, I struggled to empathize with them, especially when it came to obstacles in their work due to internal infrastructure issues. So, in order to get a sense for what they had to deal with, I attended an internal "community of practice" meetup of all mobile developers. And while I mostly expected complaints about the status quo and maybe even some bitching about product managers, I witnessed extremely self-reflective and holistic discussions. All the issues I ignorantly perceived as "excuses" had a much more fundamental impact and were already being tackled by the smartest developers in the company. After attending this meetup, my perspective on company-wide issues which we depended on completely changed. Not only was I way more aware of how to prioritize issues that would improve the work for all of us, it also turned me into an empathizing partner instead of an impatient commander.

While these kinds of experiences are incredibly rewarding and fun, you always have to remember that investing time in them is not just an occasion for baseless bragging or disproportionate ego-boosting! The idea is to send the message: "Look, I'm willing to put in the extra work to understand your domain and challenges, so I roughly know what you're dealing with on a day-to-day basis. But you'll never find me poaching onto your side of the playing field." Send this subtle message, but don't brag about (or even bring up) your achievements during daily business.

Empathy will also support you in defending and communicating team decisions to upper management—especially the difficult ones. In addition, it will feel much more natural for you to discuss technically-related delivery delays or argue about domain expert decisions.

UNDERSTANDING YOUR PEERS' OBJECTIVES

Now that you have demonstrated empathy towards your peers by starting to understand the challenges of their domains, it's time to get behind their individual objectives. Whether a team you're starting to work with is organized following traditional agile development guidelines or another form of cross-functional collaboration, you should make it a priority over the first weeks to understand the individual objectives of each team member—as well as your own underlying goals for your product. While frameworks like the mission briefing or a "Way of Working" workshop represent extrinsic motivators for everybody on the team, most of your peers' actions on a day-to-day basis are determined by internal factors.

Here's an example: you might assume that your team members want to achieve the goals you all aligned on as efficiently as possible, even if you sometimes wonder about some of their decisions. But if you observe closely you might discover that they are instead motivated to choose the newest tools and technologies to remain attractive for other jobs or conference opportunities.

Of course, patterns like this are not just limited to developers. You can find a wide range of inner motivators in all sorts of domains. For a Vice President it may mean wondering why his fellow business unit leader just doesn't prioritize her contribution to your joint operation as highly as you have. In a one-to-one situation you might find out about different KPI goals and incentive structures that are not aligned with yours.

After all, individual objectives clarify what people *say* versus what they actually *do*. People commit to a mission or process, but they are motivated by individual reasons. To work with them efficiently as a lateral leader, it helps to recognize their most important individual motivators and reverse-engineer your communication style and way of working from there.

According to Christina Wodtke and in my own experience, these are some of the most common potential motivators behind your peers' objectives:

- » Professional achievement
- » Professional pride or ethical values
- » Greater efficiency
- » Professional advancement
- » Better interpersonal relationships
- » Organizational flexibility

These kinds of drivers determine whether a designer uses a new fancy prototyping tool for the upcoming task instead of the standard one, even if that means that it takes longer.

It's important to understand these choices because they dictate *how* your peers get their job done. Look for casual one-on-one situations like coffee or lunch to get a better feeling for people's drivers. You might also be surprised how many actions are actually influenced through conversations with people managers without you being involved in them. Make sure to build rapport with the people managers of your team members so you aren't blindsided.

In her book *Radical Candor*, Kim Scott recommends a "care personally" aspect of people leadership. While you're not the one responsible for your peers' personal development, understanding how each person's job fits into their life goals is an important piece of knowledge for you as a lateral leader. Being aware of the objectives you're encountering within your team also helps when communicating disappointments and mistakes—something product managers always need to be ready for in environments with lots of agile planning changes and interdependencies with other departments. Of course, you can always go ahead and bluntly drop someone's favorite project from the roadmap. But in order to keep your team motivated for whatever comes next, you should use what you know about their motivators to explain the decision and avoid an unhealthy backlash.

Once you become aware of what makes your peers tick, it's also your responsibility as a lateral leader to put these insights into action. While there are many tactics you can utilize in your daily work with your peers (tone of voice, body language etc.), you can also create new spaces for them to own or accommodate their unique needs and interests. While some of your peers' struggles may be out of your control, one powerful approach is to discuss informal team roles that address the needs of the individual. This can't come from a people manager because they are not the ones "designing" the team and are often stuck with static job descriptions. As a lateral leader, you are empowered to shift this perspective into flexible roles for your peers.

Help your team to define and find the informal roles that match their needs, going beyond the requirements from a people manager or HR perspective. Consider how individual motivations can shape alternative roles like:

- » Facilitator
- » Mediator
- » Emotional Supporter
- » Spokesperson
- » Timekeeper
- » Office Admin

By creating these informal roles for team members, you're also shaping how that individual responds to criticism, praise, or conflict.

MEET THE AGILE PEER CANVAS

One of the biggest questions I encounter when talking to lateral leaders is how to facilitate empathy within a team. What is missing from general guidance like "Have a one-on-one coffee with people" is a structured approach to make outcomes actionable.

As I mentioned earlier, lateral leadership is about striking the balance between the business and the emotional aspects of collaboration. Both sides are partially reflected in a couple of tools that are already out there.

On one hand, there's the *Role Model Canvas* by Christian Botta. It's made for discussing gaps or overlaps between individuals within a team, but it stems from traditional project management thinking. The Role Model Canvas forces you to think about what a role or person is responsible for and what they are not. It then makes that explicit. The underlying principle of framing the role and responsibilities of individual team members is an excellent one, and provides more clarity—especially if everybody participates in defining everyone else's roles. But its weak spot lies in ignoring the emotional side of an individual by focusing primarily on job responsibilities.

On the other hand, I had good experiences in utilizing an *Empathy Map* to provide a different perspective on the needs of individual team members. While it was originally used for developing a more holistic picture of your users, it can easily be adapted for collecting and visualizing the traits of your peers. However, it can also feel a bit too vague, as it doesn't consider the process-oriented aspects of collaborating, like specific roles.

Instead, I developed my own map for making empathy visible among peers. The goal was to define a structure that would capture the business skills as well as the emotional traits of team members, bringing both aspects together and defining high-level missions as well as informal roles.

The Agile Peer Canvas.
Get it for free on herbig.blog/canvas.

The Agile Peer Canvas consists of seven areas for each team member, which I recommend working through in this order:

1. *Mission:* What's the essence of this role captured in one sentence?
2. *Do's:* What explicit tasks are clearly assigned to and owned by this person?
3. *Don'ts:* What important tasks should this person explicitly not tackle (ie. counter-examples)?
4. *Hopes:* What does this person want to get out of their role?
5. *Fears:* What is holding this person back?
6. *Drivers & Motivators:* Which aspects of this person's work make them excel and push through?
7. *Informal Role:* Which team-internal role could leverage the drivers of this person beyond their job description?

Your goal for the execution of frameworks like the Agile Peer Canvas should always be transparency. But just like product development these days, you should iterate on this. Start by filling out the Canvas on your own—either for a teammate you know pretty well or yourself. Only then should you launch your next round of a trial run—maybe involving an HR colleague and a people manager from your inner circle. When you feel that you have a draft for what might go into the sections and are confident with moderating an Agile Peer Canvas workshop involving the whole team, take the next steps:

FIRST, PLAN THE WORKSHOP WITH YOUR TEAM.
Schedule a workshop with a set of peers who form a cross-functional team on a regular basis, whether it's a task force

to tackle a new legal regulation or a classic Scrum team. The workshops will lay important groundwork for the collaboration among members in the future. Ask them to prepare at least 2–3 items per section of the Agile Peer Canvas. Share your own Canvas in advance to lead by example and lower the hurdles to getting started. Agree on rules for how to handle the shared information (e.g. not sharing with HR or people manager) to encourage openness.

SECOND, FILL IN THE CANVAS COLLABORATIVELY FOR EACH TEAM MEMBER.

When you meet for the workshop, everyone should share their self-defined Canvas with the rest of the team (agree on how to make this a safe space beforehand). Print or draw the Canvas for every team member on flip charts or whiteboards in advance. Keep this a two-sided conversation: it's not only about sharing your own thoughts but also gathering feedback from your peers on how they perceive you. To create a more holistic perspective, the other team members can suggest additional attributes for the Canvas of the presenter and can share it with her by writing down additional inputs for every aspect of this team member. Everybody shares their perspectives by putting stickies onto the Canvas. This step is the most important one in uncovering perspective gaps in terms of team roles.

THIRD, REFLECT AND ACT ON WHAT YOU HAVE LEARNED.

After the workshop, visualize the Peer Canvas outcomes on your own by organizing team members based on their emotional traits. One matrix could feature two axes:

» Less → More Business Objectives
» Less → More Emotional Objectives

By encouraging this process to take place in public, you can achieve two goals in your role as a lateral leader. First, you're now much more aware of everyone's individual drivers and what makes them tick, which builds a much more complete emotional picture of your team members. And second, you supported bonding with every other team member as well. Although not everybody will focus on developing empathy for one another like you do, chances are high that something from the empathy map of a colleague will stick.

Note: A more strategic use of these Agile Peer Canvas insights follows the scheme of Stakeholder Mapping. Using a matrix-like framework, you can visualize team members (or peers, depending on the environment you're looking at) using this background for their objectives. For example, who has a more impersonal relationship to their work environment and will therefore also mediate conflicts more objectively? This could contrast with team members who bring more emotional buy-in to the table and are more likely to start a heated discussion.

ACTIVITIES

» Ask your peers for thought leaders or blogs to follow within their domain and demonstrate genuine interest. But don't try too hard to chime in on a discussion over lunch.
» Ask if you can join the routines of a department like engineering, design, or marketing to get a sense of what matters within these communities.
» Look for opportunities to become practically involved in a domain outside your comfort zone and normal daily operational scope. For example:

- » Attend an internal or local meetup from a domain you frequently interact with (e.g. UX, iOS, or Frontend Development).
- » Take a Udemy course on how to create an artifact some of your peers are producing.
- » Write/talk about another domain from your own perspective (for example, look at the importance of continuous integration or creating style guides from a non-technical product manager's perspective).
» Schedule one-on-one coffee or lunch dates with your team members with the clear goal of talking about everything *except* day-to-day business. Figure out what brought them to their jobs in the first place.
» With permission, you can also talk to the people managers at your company for more insights into personal background, hiring history, and maybe even aspects of their career development plans.

ESCALATION: HOW TO SOLVE CONFLICTS WHEN YOU'RE NOT THE BOSS

I often get the question from product managers about what to do when lateral leadership principles fail. Unfortunately, there will always be problems that are above your pay grade or can only be achieved by applying hierarchical power. It would be naive to think that lateral leadership tools can be scaled infinitely to any problem or personality type.

And it would be outright foolish to exclude escalation from the set of tools you need in lateral leadership positions. It's important to stop avoiding conflicts because of fear of not being able to resolve them without hierarchical power. This could put team harmony and the impact of your work at risk.

There are two typical conflict situations you will face as a lateral leader:

First, with peers within your team. These could include ongoing misbehavior like ignoring team rules for working together or something more interpersonal. For these, I typically recommend having a one-on-one discussion with the team member after the third occurrence. There's plenty of great advice on how to approach these conversations in Kim Scott's book *Radical Candor*. In a nutshell, you should refer to your shared working principles and address how the team member violated them.

Second, with peers from other departments. These conflicts tend to be more on the business side of things, compared to the team internal ones. They mostly result from competing goals sent to product teams by other managers. Here, you shouldn't wait before you escalate because it's clear from the start that the two of you won't be able to resolve it. The best approach is to make this type of conflict obvious as quickly as possible to your bosses so they can make an informed decision that enables both of you to proceed.

While I think escalation is an underestimated tool when it comes to resolving conflicts among peers, it does not mean that you should escalate every conflict you encounter right away. A vast amount of conflict, whether it's hierarchical or on eye-level, should be approached through a direct conversation first. But that requires the right amount of candor in talking about the "hard things."

Because escalation is often the last resort to follow, make sure to pursue efforts for resolving the situation before you escalate.

Otherwise, you could be perceived as lazy instead of as someone who's willing to move things forward on your own. If you repeatedly and inappropriately escalate, it could also damage trust within your team.

I'll cover some common misconceptions about escalation below, but while you need to be the one who addresses these misconceptions first, it requires organizational buy-in to build a culture of what I like to call "positive escalation." If the rest of your company considers escalation to be a weakness and you encourage your peers to use it without fear, the possible blowback could create the opposite effect as managing escalation is actually about building trust.

COMMON MISCONCEPTIONS ABOUT ESCALATION
Escalation is something incredibly bad and symbolizes personal failure.
Many people associate escalation with people screaming at each other in a room. I rather recommend that you see escalation as just another a tool, like the empathy exercises or the mission briefing we discussed earlier. Don't fear it, but welcome it as an opportunity to clarify the problem and continue moving forward. In lateral discussions, I often welcomed the action of escalation, while opponents mostly considered it as a threat. Instead of becoming scared when someone threatens to escalate you should say, "I'm glad we agree on the need to escalate. May I write the email to our bosses myself?"

Conflicts can only be escalated to and solved by hierarchical leaders.
One trait of self-organized teams is to take over more and more responsibilities of what's called middle management. This can also be applied to the escalation of conflicts among peers. Remember the concept of informal roles I presented as a way to accommodate

individual motivators? How about assigning the role of the "conflict master" to one of your peers? If this person is the agreed-upon and accepted mediator, hierarchy might not be necessary here. Whether a conflict is escalated in a hierarchical or lateral way, the same rules apply (as I lay out in the escalation checklist below).

For more insights into how to design self-organized teams for complete autonomy, I recommend the illustrated version of Frederic Laloux's *Reinventing Organizations*.

Escalation is a break-up scenario, after which no further collaboration is possible.

Escalation done right is also in line with encouraging productive conflict as recommended by Amit Maimon, a VP Product and Head of R&D at ADP. First and foremost, self-managed teams must commit to openly discussing their differences. Conflict should be seen not as an annoyance that leads to anxiety and alienation, but as an opportunity for growth and strong working relationships.

By agreeing with a peer that it's now time to escalate and offering your service to provide the right format, you also lay important groundwork. After all, chances are high that the two of you will continue to work together. Why make it unnecessarily hard to maintain that professional relationship? Instead, shape and then present the escalation jointly.

Escalation means that teams depend on upper management and can't progress without them.

Keep in mind that executives are often annoyed by having to solve issues between team members. Self-organized collaboration is expected and, in general, escalation feels like babysitting. This is why it's even more important to prepare an escalation properly so it doesn't sound like "Mommy, he stole my toy and won't give it back."

Here's a great people manager's perspective on conflict management in hierarchical teams from Jeanne Brett and Stephen B. Goldberg, who are academics specializing in the field of Dispute Resolution and Mediation:

> "Why rely on mediation and not your authority? Your colleagues are more likely to own the decision and follow through with it if they're involved in making it. If you dictate what they should do, they will have learned nothing about resolving conflict themselves. Rather, they will have become more dependent on you to figure out their disputes for them."

You should keep this in mind when you arrive at a conflict situation with a lateral peer. Don't put your outcomes at risk, but also don't solely rely on your executive to solve this for you.

Escalation is a process driven by others and you can only give in and let it happen.

The most important thing about escalation is structure and objectivity. Executives (and pretty much everybody else) hate it when unstructured arguments get brought to them. Therefore, don't set up a meeting without context and just start explaining the conflict verbally. Instead, use this escalation checklist to prepare a structured email or message in which you lay out the following issues:

» The goal or action you were asked to achieve or complete (ideally referencing an aligned mission briefing)
» The best solution from your perspective to achieve that goal, including proof that you're on the right track

- » The counter-argument or conflicting goal your peer is advocating
- » Possible solutions you've discussed already and why they didn't work out
- » The one question you want your bosses to answer

Ideally, the answer comes in plain language shortly after you send the mail. Otherwise, you'll probably be asked to set up a meeting to present and resolve the argument. Don't shy away from being present in this meeting. Just as you are part of the virtual discussion by cc-ing your peer and yourself in that email, both of you should be present during the physical meeting. This demonstrates that you also own the conflict and the escalation beyond the end goal.

Escalation means someone "wins" and someone "loses."

In order to make escalation a standard tool instead of being a rare exception, it's important to think ahead to the time after the conflict has been resolved. That means accepting the resolution without holding a grudge against your peer, regardless of the outcome. After all, you want to escalate to move things forward and not to demonstrate "who's right." The cause is bigger than your own ego. While escalation may not intend to make your peer back down, sometimes that is a welcome side effect. (Some smarty-pants advice in case your solution is the one that prevails: avoid saying "I told you so" at all cost for the sake of your future relationship at work with each other.)

The more work you put into building alignment and empathy through lateral leadership, the more solid your foundation will be when it comes to escalation.

ACTIVITIES

» Practice escalating.
  » Pick a conflict you currently can't seem to resolve with a peer from within your lateral environment.
  » Talk to your peer about whether you should really bring this one level up to enable both of you to move on.
  » Collaborate with your peer on a structured outline or email for presenting the conflict to your bosses.
  » Make it very clear what action you want your respective bosses to take.

CONCLUSION

Leading people is never easy. And while this book can't make all of your pain go away as a lateral leader, it hopefully helped with five things:

» Recognizing that you have a real leadership responsibility even if the words are not in your job title
» Demonstrating why and how to break free of traditional leadership thinking when it comes to leading peers at eye-level
» Ensuring alignment on your vision with team members and peers by making use of an agreed-upon format like the mission briefing instead of relying on implicit assumptions
» Developing the right amount of empathy for recognizing the challenges your peers struggle with at work
» Acknowledging that you should not shy away from escalation but embrace it when necessary

Leading without hierarchical power is hard. But even if you may sometimes yearn to give top-down commands, think of the downside of working with people who only follow orders.

Be the leader you want to follow yourself.

READING LIST

Bezos, Jeff. 2016 Letter to Shareholders (2017). https://blog.aboutamazon.com/company-news/2016-letter-to-shareholders

Bhat, Nilima, and Raj Sisodia. "Why 'feminine' traits lead to higher revenue, performance and customer engagement" (2018). https://www.hotjar.com/humans/feminine-traits-in-business-leadership-with-raj-sisodia-nilima-bhat

Bielaszka-DuVernay, Christina. "How to Lead When You're Not the Boss" (2009). https://hbr.org/2009/02/how-to-lead-when-youre-not-the

Botta, Christian. "Role Model Canvas—Die visuelle RACI-Alternative" (2016). https://de.linkedin.com/pulse/role-model-canvas-die-visuelle-raci-alternative-christian-botta

Brett, Jeanne, and Stephen B. Goldberg. "How to Handle a Disagreement on Your Team" (2017). https://hbr.org/2017/07/how-to-handle-a-disagreement-on-your-team

Bungay, Stephen. *The Art of Action: How Leaders Close the Gaps between Plans, Actions and Results* (2010).

Cancel, David. "Scaling the Unscalable: How 1-to-1 conversations with customers help Drift grow" (2018). https://www.hotjar.com/humans/how-customer-conversations-help-drift-grow-with-david-cancel

Chu, Brandon. "Product Management Mental Models for Everyone" (2018). https://blackboxofpm.com/product-management-mental-models-for-everyone-31e7828cb50b

Crandell, Rich. "Empathy Map" (2010). https://dschool-old.stanford.edu/groups/k12/wiki/3d994/empathy_map.html

Doyle, Andy. "Management and Organization at Medium" (2016). https://blog.medium.com/management-and-organization-at-medium-2228cc9d93e9

Eriksson, Martin. "What, Exactly, is a Product Manager?" (2011). https://www.mindtheproduct.com/2011/10/what-exactly-is-a-product-manager/

Greenleaf, Robert K., and Larry C. Spears. *Servant Leadership: A Journey into the Nature of Legitimate Power and Greatness* (2002).

Hamel, Gary. *The Future of Management* (2007).

Hedges, Kristi. "5 Questions to Help Your Employees Find Their Inner Purpose" (2017). https://hbr.org/2017/08/5-questions-to-help-your-employees-find-their-inner-purpose

Hemphill, Courtney. "How to Promote Psychological Safety on Your Team" (2018). https://blog.carbonfive.com/2018/06/05/how-to-promote-psychological-safety-on-your-team/

Hogan, Lara. "Team Leader Venn Diagram" (2018). https://medium.com/making-meetup/em-el-pm-venn-diagram-764e79b42baf

Horowitz, Ben. *The Hard Thing about Hard Things* (2014).

Kadish, Marc. "Collaborative Alignment – the 'Auftragsklärung' framework" (2016). https://www.mindtheproduct.com/2016/08/alignment-framework-managing-stakeholder-communications/

Kittler, Arne. "Product Culture in a Growing Organization" (2017). https://www.slideshare.net/ArneKittler/product-culture-in-a-growing-organization-productized-conference-2017-81848814

Kniberg, Hendrik. "Scrum Checklist" (2012). https://www.crisp.se/gratis-material-och-guider/scrum-checklist

Knight, Rebecca. "How to Increase Your Influence at Work" (2018). https://hbr.org/2018/02/how-to-increase-your-influence-at-work

Laloux, Frederic. *Reinventing Organizations: An Illustrated Invitation to Join the Conversation on Next-Stage Organizations* (2016).

Leto, Kate. "Manage Conflict by Building Your Product EQ" (2018). https://www.mindtheproduct.com/2018/03/manage-conflict-building-your-product-eq/

Maimon, Amit. "How Self-Managed Teams Can Resolve Conflict" (2017). https://hbr.org/2017/04/how-self-managed-teams-can-resolve-conflict

Manageris Synopses. "The keys to lateral leadership" (2010). https://www.manageris.com/synopsis-the-keys-to-lateral-leadership-20370.html

Manifesto for Agile Software Development (2001). http://agilemanifesto.org/

Marcus, Bob. "Evolving Leadership: From Command-and-Control to Engage-and-Align" (2018). https://www.linkedin.com/pulse/evolving-leadership-from-command-and-control-bob-marcus

Palizban, Amin. "Motivate Your Team Intrinsically Or Extrinsically?" (2011). https://7geese.com/intrinsic-vs-extrinsic-motivation/

Partogi, Joshua. "What is Servant Leadership" (2017). https://www.scrum.org/resources/blog/what-servant-leadership

Pedersen, Carsten Lund, and Thomas Ritter. "Great Corporate Strategies Thrive on the Right Amount of Tension" (2017). https://hbr.org/2017/11/great-corporate-strategies-thrive-on-the-right-amount-of-tension

Perkin, Neil. "Aligned Autonomy" (2018). http://www.onlydeadfish.co.uk/only_dead_fish/2018/02/aligned-autonomy.html

Pichler, Roman. "Should Product Owners be Servant-Leaders?" (2016). https://www.romanpichler.com/blog/should-product-owners-be-servant-leaders/

Prentice, W.C.H. "Understanding Leadership" (2004). https://hbr.org/2004/01/understanding-leadership

Scott, Bill. "6 Principles for Enabling Build/Measure/Learn: Lean Engineering in Action" (2013). https://www.slideshare.net/billwscott/6-principles-for-enabling-buildmeasurelearn-lean-engineering-in-action/54-agile_doesnt_have_a_brainagile

Scott, Kim. *Radical Candor: How to Get What You Want by Saying What You Mean* (2017).

Stout-Rostron, Sunny. *Business Coaching International: Transforming Individuals and Organizations* (2014).

Vallacher, Robin R., and Daniel M. Wegner. "Action Identification Theory" (2014).
https://www.researchgate.net/profile/Robin_Vallacher/publication/229061776_Action_Identification_Theory/links/09e41502a79952946b000000/Action-Identification-Theory.pdf

Williamson, Cheryl. "Servant Leadership: How to Put Your People Before Yourself" (2017).
https://www.forbes.com/sites/forbescoachescouncil/2017/07/19/servant-leadership-how-to-put-your-people-before-yourself/

Wodtke, Christina. "Beyond OKRs: The Formula for High Performing Teams" (2017). http://eleganthack.com/beyond-okrs-the-formula-for-high-performing-teams/

Wodtke, Christina. "Using OKRs to Increase Organizational Learning" (2018). http://eleganthack.com/using-okrs-to-increase-organizational-learning/

XING. "Auftragsklärung" (2018). https://auftragsklaerung.com/

ACKNOWLEDGMENTS

First, thanks to Josh Seiden, Jeff Gothelf, and Vicky Olsen at Sense and Respond Press. I had the pleasure of getting to know Jeff during a workshop at XING a couple of years ago and have since then been an avid follower of his work. So, when the opportunity opened up to collaborate with him on the topic of lateral leadership, I knew that this needed to happen.

My ability to build great products and successfully lead agile teams has been the result of incredible mentors I worked with and for during the past eight years. First, during my time at Gruner+Jahr, Christian Hasselbring introduced me to the world of product management at scale and, more importantly, empathetic leadership for one another. Later on, Lars Neumann helped me to understand the essentials of thinking and working Agile, which left me hungry for more.

My time at XING was the one that influenced my career the most and also allowed me to connect with incredible professionals whom I'm now fortunate to call friends. Moreover, I couldn't have asked for better leaders to learn from then Patrick Roelofs and Moritz Kothe. They challenged me to continually step out of my comfort zone and rethink my perspectives, which allowed me to grow professionally and personally more than I could have imagined.

Thanks also to beta readers Christian Becker, Florian Gansemer, Thomas Leitermann, and Marcus Wermuth, whose feedback and perspective helped me to craft this book.

Finally, and most importantly, my significant other Sonja and our beloved son Jannis. To Sonja, for being my most honest critic, my biggest fan, and for being the one I can rely on when things get tough. And to Jannis, for reminding me every day of what truly matters.

TIM HERBIG is a product and business leader, as well as a prolific author and speaker. Over the past eight years, he held product leadership roles at large-scale companies such as XING and Gruner+Jahr, as well as multiple startups in the SaaS and social network space. He also co-organizes the Product Tank Hamburg meetup to promote the local product management community.

www.herbigt.com
🐦 @herbigt
📷 @herbigt
in herbigt

Made in the USA
Las Vegas, NV
17 January 2021